PANORAMAS
RAIN FOREST

BackPackBooks
·
NEW YORK

CONTENTS

RAIN FORESTS OF THE WORLD

Tropical rain forests are found near the equator, in regions of high rainfall. The main areas are in the Amazon basin of South America, Central America, central and west Africa, Southeast Asia, and eastern Madagascar. There are also small areas of rain forest in northern Australia and the Pacific Islands.

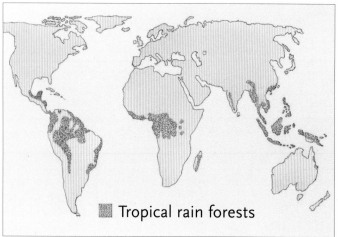

Tropical rain forests

4

LEOPARD

GORILLA

PYTHON

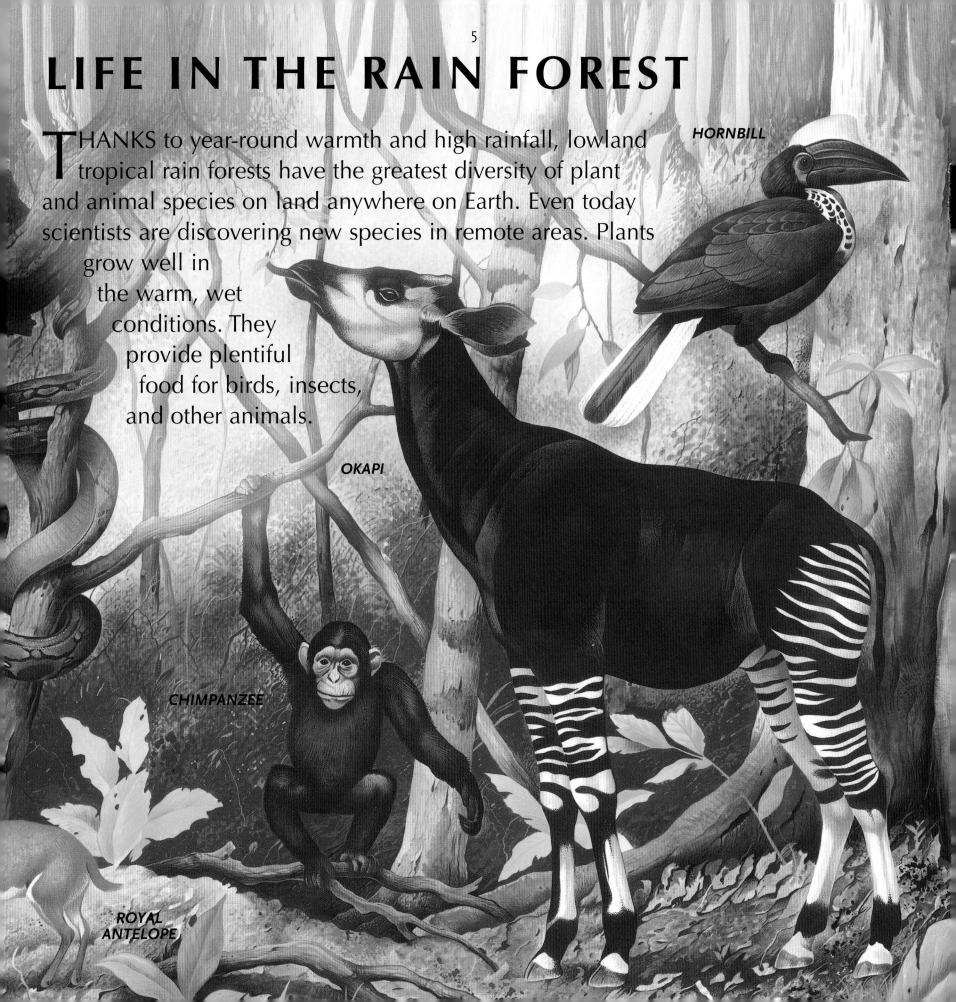

LIFE IN THE RAIN FOREST

HORNBILL

THANKS to year-round warmth and high rainfall, lowland tropical rain forests have the greatest diversity of plant and animal species on land anywhere on Earth. Even today scientists are discovering new species in remote areas. Plants grow well in the warm, wet conditions. They provide plentiful food for birds, insects, and other animals.

OKAPI

CHIMPANZEE

ROYAL ANTELOPE

FRUIT BATS

BLUE-RUMPED PARROT

WESTERN TARSIER

SIAMANG GIBBON

SONGSTERS

Each dawn, the peace of the rain forest is broken by the call of the gibbon. These are often elaborate "songs" that, in some species, sound like operatic solos or duets! Males have throat sacs that help amplify their voices. Gibbons swing through the trees using their long arms and hooked hands.

GREAT MEMNON BUTTERFLY

SILVERED LANGUR

FLYING MAMMALS

The Southeast Asian rain forest is home to many different species of bat, the only mammals that can truly fly. Most are insect-eating bats, which hunt their prey at night using echolocation. But some are fruit bats, thriving on the year-round supply of fruit and flowers.

GLIDERS

The easiest way to get from one tree to another in the forest is to fly—or glide. The colugo, or flying lemur, has a loose flap of skin between its neck, limbs, and tail, which enables it to glide for huge distances while losing very little height. The gliding frog uses the webbing between its toes like tiny parachutes. The flying dragon, a kind of lizard, has skin flaps like wings.

IN THE RAIN FOREST TREES
Southeast Asian rain forest

LIFE in the rain forest is organized into several layers, like the stories of a building. The highest stories are the trees that grow taller than the other trees around them. These are known as emergent trees. Beneath the emergent layer is the canopy, a near-continuous "roof" made up of tree foliage. Bathed in sunlight, plants and flowers take root on the branches themselves. These are called epiphytes. Many animals, including apes, monkeys, butterflies, and birds, make their home in the canopy. Lower down is the understory, where some animals glide from tree to tree. Here too is the domain of the leopard. It waits on branches for its prey to pass on the ground below.

CRESTED SWIFTS

WHISKERED TREESWIFT

RED-BEARDED BEE-EATER

GREAT HORNBILL

COLUGO

BIRDS OF THE RAIN FOREST

FROM the tiny hummingbird, hovering over flowers to feed on nectar, to the harpy eagle, a fearsome bird of prey, the Amazon rain forest is rich with birdlife. The scarlet macaw's strong beak can crack open even the hardest nuts, while the toco toucan uses its huge bill to pick fruits. On the forest floor, curassows scratch around for fruits and seeds. At the river's edge, the sunbittern wades in search of fish and small crustaceans while a kingfisher waits to dive for its fish supper.

The untidy nest of the hoatzin looks as if it may fall apart at any moment. By contrast, the long hanging nest of the cacique is carefully woven.

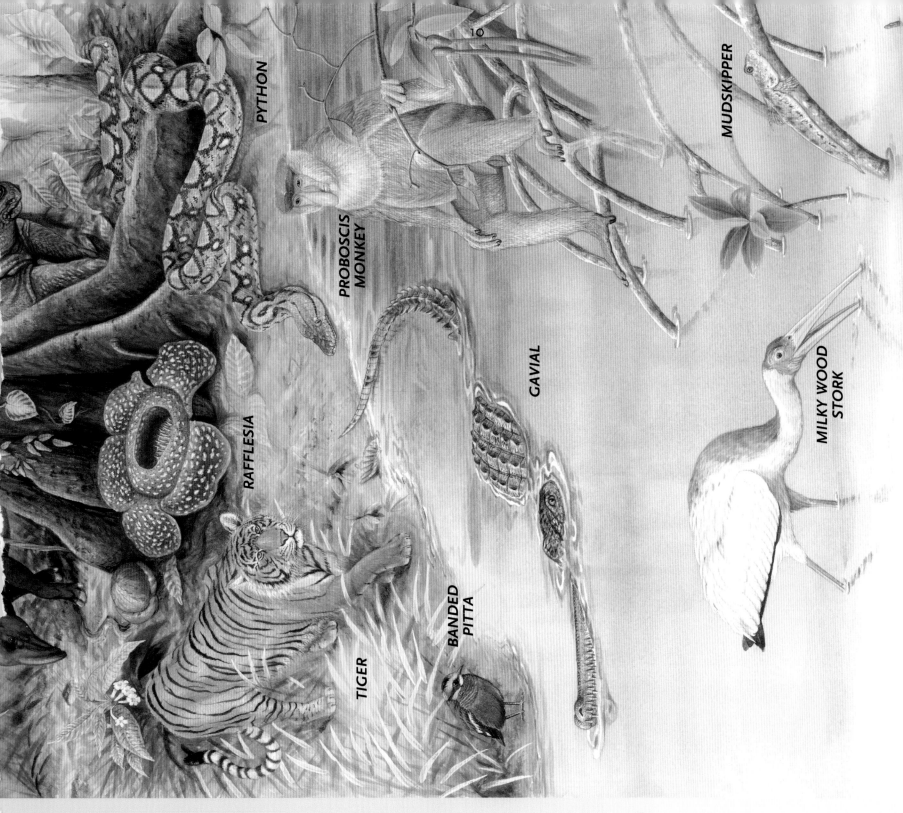

PYTHON

PROBOSCIS MONKEY

MUDSKIPPER

RAFFLESIA

GAVIAL

MILKY WOOD STORK

TIGER

BANDED PITTA

10

GROUND DWELLERS

On the ground, fungi grow, fallen leaves collect, and tiny shoots push through. The tapir searches for water plants at night. Both Sumatran rhinoceroses and tigers are now very rare, due to the disappearance of their forest habitat and to hunting. The proboscis monkey, named after the male's long, fat nose, lives among the branches of mangrove trees, feeding on fruit and leaves.

FISH OUT OF WATER

There is a kind of fish that spends most of its life out of water. The mudskipper makes its home on the mudflats. It skips about on the soft mud using its flippers and fins, even climbing trees with the help of a sucker on its underside.

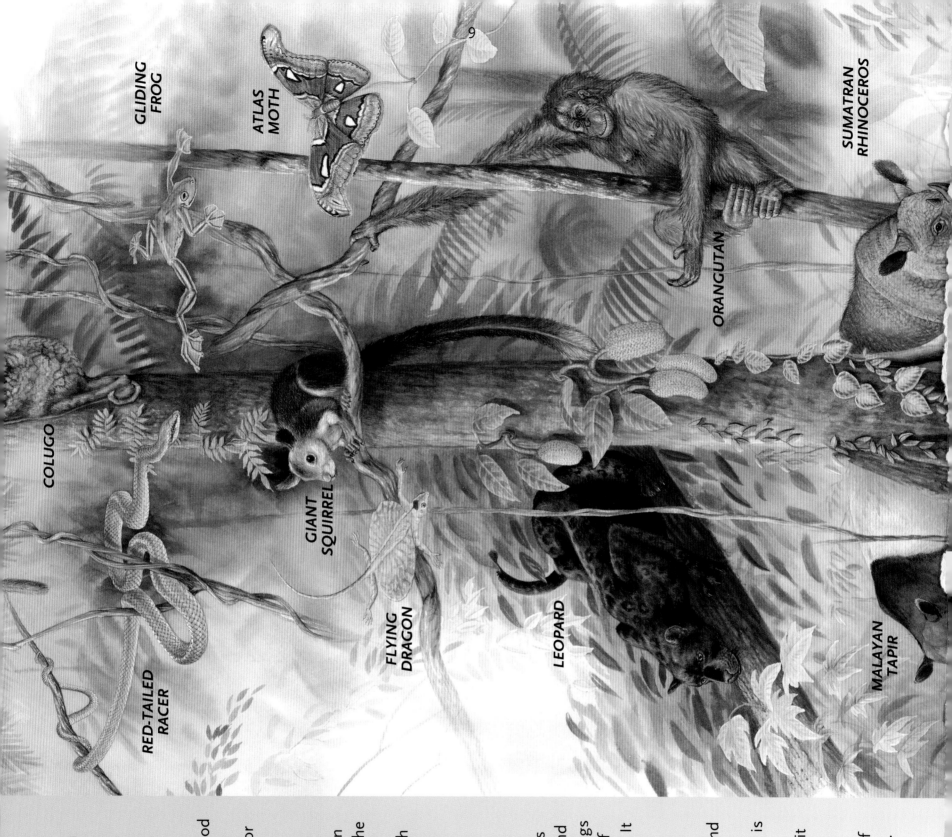

GLIDING FROG

ATLAS MOTH

SUMATRAN RHINOCEROS

ORANGUTAN

COLUGO

GIANT SQUIRREL

FLYING DRAGON

RED-TAILED RACER

LEOPARD

MALAYAN TAPIR

LEAPERS

Primates get from tree to tree by leaping. Tarsiers move around the branches only at night. Their huge eyes give them good vision in the dark, while they listen for insects with their dishlike ears. The silvered langur is equally at home on the ground or in the trees. Pushing off from a branch with great force, it can leap up to 10 feet.

LONERS

The orangutan has shaggy red hair and long arms. It swings cautiously by itself through the trees. It has a good knowledge of the forest and always knows where to find its favorite fruit trees. The leopard is another loner. Hunting at night, it carefully stalks its prey with its excellent senses of hearing and smell.

PEOPLE OF THE RAIN FOREST

MANY native peoples of the rain forest still follow a way of life that has remained unchanged for centuries. Some travel through the forest, making temporary camps. Others live in established villages and grow crops in forest clearings. Native peoples depend on the forest for their survival. They hunt for animals among the trees or catch fish and turtles in the rivers. They gather fruits and seeds and make canoes from hollowed-out trees.

KAYAPO INDIAN

This Kayapo Indian *(below)* wears a plate stuck into his lower lip. Like many Amazon peoples, his way of life is under threat. As parts of the forest disappear, native people leave to work in cities. Guns and outboard motors have also changed the way the Indians hunt and get about.

BOW AND ARROW

Many Amazon Indians still use bows and arrows or blowpipe darts to hunt or fish. The arrowheads are carved from twigs, bones, or scrap metal. By coating the tips with poison from certain kinds of frogs, the Indians may kill their prey instantly.

SNAKE HUNTERS

The anaconda, of the Amazon rain forest, rarely attacks humans. All the same, it is hunted by the Indians, who use blowpipe darts or rifles to kill it. Several men are needed to carry its body back to the village: a large anaconda weighs more than a cow!

Then they weave the branches together to form a dome-shaped frame (3) which they cover with leaves (4). Traditional huts made from natural materials are still used by hunter-gatherers in other parts of the world.

EFE PYGMIES

The Efe pygmies live in the rain forests of central Africa. They travel around hunting animals and collecting honey. At night they make huts to shelter in. First they mark out a circle in the ground (1) and drive branches into the ground round the circle (2).

WORKING WITH ELEPHANTS

Asian elephants are still used in Southeast Asia to clear forest and move logs. The elephants are trained to lift and drag logs following voice commands. Rain-forest logging was banned in Thailand in 1990. Now the elephants and their handlers, called mahouts, work in the tourist industry, taking people on rides.

CITIES IN THE RAIN FOREST

The Maya people live in the rain forests of Central America. A great Maya civilization rose in the period 300 B.C. to A.D. 250—about the same time as the Roman Empire in Europe. The Maya people cleared large areas of forest, drained swamps, and built huge temple-pyramids, palaces, and cities. Hundreds of years later, their civilization collapsed. The buildings crumbled and became covered over by thick forest.

TAPIR

The tapir uses its strong body to push through dense jungle. Usually active only at night, it stays close to rivers, browsing on leaves, shoots, and twigs. It pulls them toward its mouth with its short trunk. To avoid the attention of jaguars, the tapir keeps on the move. Its sense of smell helps warn of danger.

BRAZILIAN TAPIR

FISH

The largest of all Amazon fish, the pirarucu grows to 12 feet or more in length. It prefers shallow, swampy water to spawn in. It has a swim bladder, a kind of "lung" that it uses to breathe air when its head is above water. Like the pirarucu, the arawana preys on insects and other fish. It will often leap right out of the water to take them. It has even been known to snatch birds off branches!

HUMMINGBIRDS

POSTMAN BUTTERFLY

JACANA

PIRANHAS

ARAWANA

FEEDING FRENZY

The piranha is armed with razor-sharp teeth. Schools of 20 or more piranhas will, on detecting blood in the water, set about an injured animal, reducing anything the size of a pig to a mere skeleton in a very short time. Normally, the piranha feeds on small fish and fruit.

ELECTRIC EEL

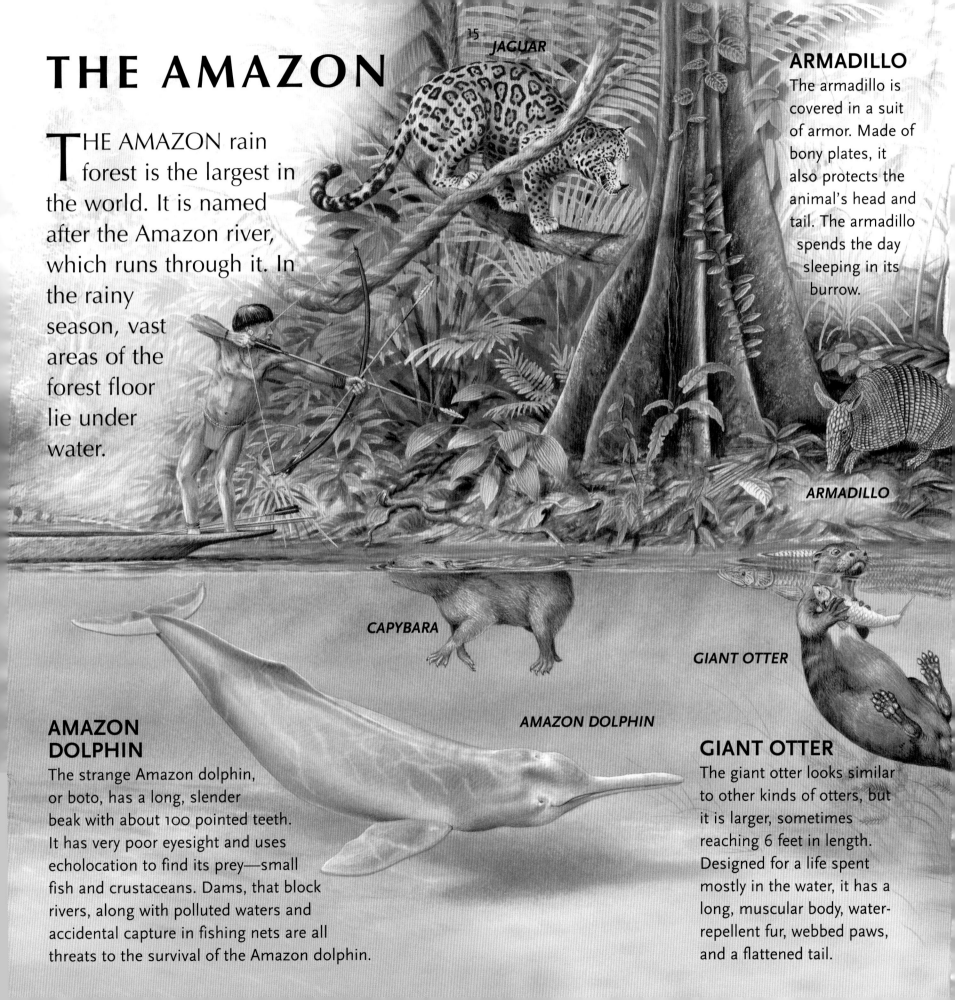

THE AMAZON

THE AMAZON rain forest is the largest in the world. It is named after the Amazon river, which runs through it. In the rainy season, vast areas of the forest floor lie under water.

JAGUAR

ARMADILLO

The armadillo is covered in a suit of armor. Made of bony plates, it also protects the animal's head and tail. The armadillo spends the day sleeping in its burrow.

ARMADILLO

CAPYBARA

GIANT OTTER

AMAZON DOLPHIN

AMAZON DOLPHIN

The strange Amazon dolphin, or boto, has a long, slender beak with about 100 pointed teeth. It has very poor eyesight and uses echolocation to find its prey—small fish and crustaceans. Dams, that block rivers, along with polluted waters and accidental capture in fishing nets are all threats to the survival of the Amazon dolphin.

GIANT OTTER

The giant otter looks similar to other kinds of otters, but it is larger, sometimes reaching 6 feet in length. Designed for a life spent mostly in the water, it has a long, muscular body, water-repellent fur, webbed paws, and a flattened tail.

JUNGLE BUGS

RAIN FORESTS teem with insects and other minibeasts. They thrive in the hot, damp climate where there is a plentiful supply of flowers and fruit. A single tree may be home to several thousand different species of insect. Insect eaters, such as ants, wasps, birds, and lizards, are also abundant. To avoid being eaten by predators, many insects are camouflaged or have bright warning colors, indicating that they are poisonous.

ADVANCING ARMY

Army ants *(below)* march steadily through the Central and South American rain forest undergrowth killing anything in their path. One colony may consist of hundreds of thousands of ants, and they form a pack that can be 30 feet wide.

MORPHO BUTTERFLY

The blue morpho butterfly *(below)* lives in the rain forests of Central and South America. Its wings measure 6 inches across. It lives as an adult butterfly for just two weeks. It feeds mainly on plant sap and the juice of rotting fruit.

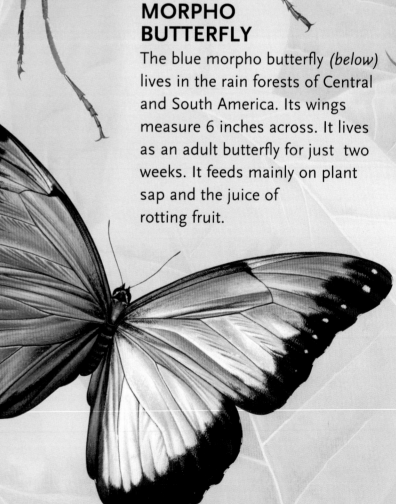

HISSING COCKROACH

The hissing cockroach *(above)* can measure up to 3 inches long. It lives in the rain forest on the Indian Ocean island of Madagascar. It has a very unusual way of protecting itself. When threatened, it fills with air to look bigger and then forces the air out with a loud hissing sound.

BIRDWING BUTTERFLY

Birdwing butterflies *(right)*, from the rain forests of Southeast Asia, are the largest butterflies of all. However, only the males show off these beautiful green, yellow, and orange tones. Female birdwings are a dull brown color.

CENTIPEDE

The giant Malayan centipede *(below)* can grow up to 8 inches long. It can run quickly, and it has massive jaws with a venomous bite for good measure! Its diet includes lizards and mice.

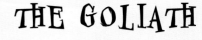

THE GOLIATH

The goliath beetle, from the central African rain forest, is one of the biggest beetles in the world: it can weigh as much as a rat. In spite of this huge weight, it can still fly into the treetops looking for fruit to eat. At night, it crawls under leaves to hide from lizards and other predators.

BUSH CRICKET

The bush cricket *(right)* lives in the Amazon rain forest. When still, it looks like a dead leaf, but if disturbed it launches itself into the air. Its wings unfold and reveal colored eyespots to startle its attacker.

HAWKMOTH

Hawkmoths *(right)* have the longest tongues in the insect world. All butterflies and moths have tubelike tongues for sucking nectar from flowers. This hawkmoth's tongue must be long enough to reach inside a certain kind of orchid.

IGUANAS

Iguanas are kinds of lizards. The green iguana has a crest of comblike spikes running down its back. If danger threatens, it will simply drop out of the trees into the water below. The green anole, another kind of iguana, has long toe pads to help it grip to tree trunks. The male's red throat flap is used in displays to attract females.

FROGS AND TOADS

Some tree frogs climb high up into the trees. They carry their tadpoles on their backs, searching out hollows where water has collected. Here the tadpoles develop into adults. The Suriname toad also carries its young on its back—in special pockets. This unusual toad has a flat, square body, webbed hind feet, and star-shaped fingertips.

MORPHO BUTTERFLY

GREEN ANOLE

GREEN IGUANA

TREE FROG

SURINAME TOAD

ARRAU TURTLE

SPECTACLED CAIMAN

CAIMAN

The caiman lurks in shallow water with just its eyes and nostrils showing. When a tapir or capybara comes to drink, it seizes it in its teeth and drags it under water.

MATAMATA

The matamata lurks on the riverbed, waiting for fish to approach. The flaps on the skin on its neck wave in the water, attracting the fish's curiosity. Then the matamata suddenly thrusts out its neck, opens its vast mouth, and swallows the fish in one gulp.

MATAMATA

HYACINTH
MACAW

INSECTS

Leafcutter ants cut out pieces of leaf, which they carry back to their nests. There they grow fungus "gardens" on the leaf pieces, which provide the ants with their food. The butterflies' bright colors protect them from birds by providing camouflage or to warn predators that they are poisonous. Large eyespots may also scare attackers away.

BEWARE: SPIDERS

Bird-eating spiders hunt at night when they lie in wait for passing insects, frogs, or lizards (but seldom birds). They inject venom into their prey through large fangs. The paralyzed animal is squirted with digestive juices to turn its insides to liquid. The spider then sucks out its insides.

LEAFCUTTER
ANTS

OWL
BUTTERFLY

BIRD-EATING
SPIDER

SUNBITTERN

ANACONDA

AMAZON
KINGFISHER

TETRAS

PIRARUCU

ANACONDA

At more than 30 feet long, the anaconda is one of the world's longest and heaviest snakes. It seizes its prey by the neck and coils its body around it to suffocate the animal to death. It then swallows its victim whole.

ENDANGERED FOREST

MORE AND MORE rain forest is being destroyed due to logging and clearances for ranching, agriculture, quarrying, and roads. A number of well-known animals and plants are seriously threatened with extinction as their rain forest habitats are bulldozed away, and as hunting continues unchecked. Where some kinds of animals, such as the orangutan or tiger, were once to be found in the hundreds of thousands, populations are now down to a few hundred. It can only be a short time before these animals become extinct in the wild forever.

ORANGUTAN
Tree felling in Indonesia has deprived orangutans of much of their habitat. They are now confined to small areas of rain forest in Borneo and Sumatra.

JAVAN RHINOCEROS

Rhinoceroses are killed just for their horns, which are used as medicines in the Far East. Only about 60 rhinoceroses native to the island of Java, Indonesia, survive today.

AYE-AYE

The aye-aye feeds on fruit and grubs in the Madagascan rain forest. It uses its long, thin middle fingers to scrape out grubs from behind the bark of trees. It is very rare, due to habitat loss and persecution from local residents, who believe it murders people while they sleep.

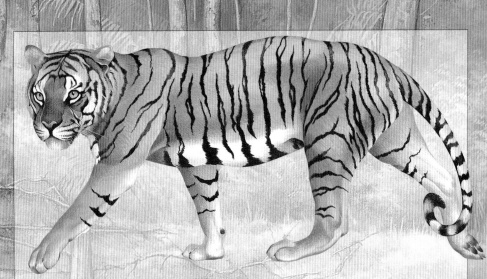

TIGER

The trade in animal skins to make fur coats or rugs has drastically reduced the number of tigers in the wild. In India, reserves have been set up with wardens who guard the animals against poachers.

GLOSSARY

CAMOUFLAGE The means by which living things escape the notice of predators (or prey, when they themselves are predators) by using their colors or patterns to blend into their surroundings.

CANOPY The mass of foliage in the upper part of trees. In the rain forest, foliage of trees growing close together forms an almost continuous "roof." Very little sunlight gets through to the ground. The canopy is rich in all forms of life, including birds, flowers, monkeys and apes, insects, and bats.

ECHOLOCATION The process of sending out sounds (often too high-pitched for humans to hear) and locating the position of objects from the echoes heard back. An animal can build up a detailed picture of its surroundings entirely from the way objects reflect sound. Many kinds of whales, dolphins, and bats practice echolocation. A bat can even pinpoint insects in this way.

EPIPHYTE A plant that grows on another plant and has no roots in the soil. It obtains nutrients from rainwater, moss, and accumulated debris, such as leaf litter. Tropical rain forest epiphytes include orchids, bromeliads, and ferns.

EQUATOR The imaginary circle around the Earth's surface exactly midway between the North and South Poles. Tropical rain forests are always found near the Equator.

HABITAT The type of surroundings in which a plant or animal lives.

MANGROVE A kind of tree that grows in the muddy swamps along tropical coasts or estuaries. It has roots set aboveground so that they can take in oxygen from the air. The roots are submerged under saltwater at high tide.

PREDATOR An animal that obtains its food by hunting and attacking other animals.

PRIMATES The group of mammals that includes tarsiers, lemurs, monkeys, apes, and humans. Primates have hands and feet designed for grasping branches and nails instead of claws. They have large brains and good eyesight for judging distance.

RAIN FOREST A forest that has a great deal of rain all year round. Tropical rain forests are found near the Equator. Plants grow quickly in the warm, lush environment. More kinds of animals and plants live in tropical rain forests than anywhere else on land.